THE WATCHMAKER AND TIME

DEVANG KANAVIA

EMBASSY BOOKS
www.embassybooks.in

This edition first published in 2018

Published in India by:
Embassy Book Distributors
120, Great Western Building,
Maharashtra Chamber of Commerce Lane,
Fort, Mumbai - 400 023.
Tel : (91-22) 22819546 / 22818567.
Email : info@embassybooks.in
Website : www.embassybooks.in

Distribution Centres:
Mumbai, Bangalore, Kolkata, Chennai,
Hyderabad, New Delhi, Pune

ISBN: 978-93-86450-98-2

Page Design and Layout by PSV Kumarasamy

Printed and Bound in India by Repro India Ltd., India

Contents

Part One

The Question

If there was nothing to search for,
what would the mind do?

She made herself comfortable in the big chair. It was nearly double her size, placed right in front of the watchmaker's working table. She gazed around the room, almost sinking into the huge chair. It was one of the biggest rooms in the house. The watchmaker had named it his *Time Library*.

It held his collection of the unique clocks he had picked up from across the globe. Anyone entering the room for the first time was sure to be left speechless looking at the exceptional compendium. All watches were exclusive in their designs and had only one thing in common. The time. With all clock hands moving together at the same time, it presented a rhythmic orchestrated motion. They rightfully said that *it was difficult to keep track of time in Pedro's Time Library.*

She never missed a chance to sneak a quick glance into this room whenever she visited him. She adored looking at the variety of clocks displayed. She would sit down, count them all and then try guessing the new additions to the collection.

This time her attention was caught by an antique timepiece. It was a little red cuckoo clock, which seemed lost amongst the clutter of the big ones towering around it. The sight of the cuckoo clock brought an instant smile to her lips. But her smile vanished within no time. His stern instructions were hovering over her mind.

'No movement, no noise, until her watch was ready.'

Her eyes instantly rolled to check if he had noticed her smile.

He was busy. When he had a watch to work on, the world stopped existing for him. He was born to work with watches. The complexities in watches were his battlefields. And till date, he had never lost a battle. It could be the toughest of squads defending the issues within the watch, he would combat them all and get the watch back into the hands of time.

Fifteen minutes had passed since he started his little battle on her watch. He was so engrossed that he hadn't even once raised his head. Losing focus for him meant losing time to opponents. Little did he know that it was his final battle with his opponents; his destiny had a bigger battle in store for him; a battle, which he had not dared to confront all his life.

He sat at his table in the center of the room, undeterred. With the magnifying glass fixed to his eye, head bent over the watch, his hands swiftly shifted through the tools and the tiny elements of the watch.

She raised her head a little, to take a peek at his toolkit. It had some of the best tools in the world, most of them designed by him. Each piece was a work of art. She wished she could play with them. But playing was too farfetched; he wouldn't even let her touch them!

Sitting motionless in one place and that too without uttering a single word, she was now getting restless. In a room full of clocks, time seemed to have lost its pace. She was trying hard to think of things she could do being seated there. *'The Flipbook!'* The thought brought a sly grin to her face. She was carrying a little flipbook in her purse. She slowly picked up her purse and placed it on her lap. She seemed happy to have accomplished it without making even the slightest of noises. But the next task of opening the zipped purse with the same precision was actually the difficult one. She took a deep breath, closed her eyes, raised her shoulders gently and slowly pulled the zip. The zip had a mind of its own. It let out a sharp sound breaking the silence in the room. Embarrassed and scared, she slowly opened her eyes. He was still working, oblivious to the world around him. She grinned, relieved at not having disturbed him.

Before a second thought could pass her mind, he interrupted, "Maria, I asked you not to make any noise. Stop playing with your bag." He made his point clear. He didn't even raise his head while saying this, but it was enough to drive her smile away.

This was it. She couldn't take it anymore. "How much more time, Grandpa? Why is it taking ages? Can it even be repaired?"

The magnifying glass resting on his eye popped out and fell on the table. It rolled for a while before coming to a halt. The watchmaker raised his head; the curly white hair springing on his head taking their time to settle.

There was anger written all over his face. This was enough to indicate to Maria that she had crossed the line. Before she could utter something to undo the damage, he responded in a curt manner. "There is no watch in this world that can't be repaired by Pedro. They don't call your Grandpa, '*The Maestro of Time*', for no reason." Her eyes went wide. "Here, your watch is done." He waved his hand asking her to come and check for herself.

She kept her purse aside, ran and stretched her palm in front of him. He steadily placed her watch on it. Looking at the hands of her watch go in tandem with the rest of its peers in the room, her smile was back where it belonged. "Wow, Grandpa! This is amazing. It's working. You are truly a *Maestro*. Thank you."

He lifted her and made her sit on the table. She was busy wearing her watch.

"Grandpa, do you remember you gifted this watch to me two years back?"

"Yes, I do. It was your sixth birthday then, wasn't it?"

"Yes. And my first watch."

"Hmmm. Red like your rosy cheeks. You know, I had gifted a similar one to your mom when she was your age. I had to search in a lot of places to get the same model for you."

"Even Ma has the same watch? She never told me." Her disappointment instantly showed up in her eyes. "Wait," She almost pounced back recollecting something, "She has a different watch. It isn't red. It is silver. And it was given to her by dad."

Pedro couldn't stop laughing, "Maria! Maria! I gave it to her when she was a little girl like you. Now that watch wouldn't even be working. It must be lying in one of your mom's old boxes."

"Her time also stopped working?"

He burst out laughing. "Time doesn't stop, sweetheart. Only a watch stops working," his laughter echoed in the house.

"Stop laughing." She pulled the bottom of his shirt, feeling annoyed. "When Dad asks Ma what time it is, she looks at the watch and tells him the time. A watch means time. Isn't it? Then, why are you laughing?"

He hadn't laughed like this in years. Laughter was never a part of his serious demeanor. Even his closest acquaintances wouldn't have seen him laughing so openly.

He got a little serious in his manner sensing the

irritation in her tone. "A watch and time are different, Maria. A watch only shows time. It is not time."

She looked puzzled.

"Now, how do I explain it to you?" He looked around searching for something that he could use to clarify her doubt. He saw her purse and asked what she was carrying in it.

"My identy card, my pocket mirror, my lipstick, my kerchief and my new flipbook."

"It is an '*identity*' card, not identy card," he corrected her. "And you carry a lipstick too? You are a big girl now. Hmmm!" He commented playfully.

She raised her chin with pride but felt a little shy at the same time.

"Does your identity card have your school address on it?"

"Yes. Saint Blaise High School. 14th lane, behind Sonora Fountain."

"That's very good. So now tell me. Are the school and address different or the same? Is this the address or your school?"

"My address is here, but my school is far. The address

only tells where my school is. The address is not the school. You don't know anything Grandpa." She slapped her forehead.

"You are right, Maria. Sometimes, because of my old age, I forget simple things." He chuckled and gave her a pat. "Now you see, a watch also only tells you the time. A watch is not time. Do you now understand?" He felt he had accomplished a big task successfully.

But Maria looked all the more confused. She was somehow still finding it difficult to understand. Although she nodded in agreement, her eyes spoke differently.

He couldn't have done it better than this, Pedro told himself. Just as he moved to put the tools in the toolbox, he heard her voice, "I know where my school is. But where is time?"

"What?" The question almost cut the ground from under his feet. Pedro left his tools alone and turned around.

She repeated thinking that maybe she wasn't clear the first time. "If the watch only shows what time it is, then where is this 'time'?"

"Huh! Maria! Don't ask stupid questions, ok? I have work. Off you go." He lifted her and let her off the table. And patted her head as he opened the door for her.

He turned towards his tools but felt morose at having escaped the discussion by pushing her away. She had only taken a few steps before he called her back. "Wait."

He made her sit on the table again and seated himself on the chair facing her. She sat clutching her purse as he closed his eyes deliberating on what to say. He summoned up all his views and tried putting the complex subject in the simplest of forms to make her understand.

"You see Maria, time is everywhere. In fact, we are in time and moving with time. You've sat in an airplane. Haven't you?"

She nodded in excitement.

"Time is like a big airplane, and we all are sitting in it. You can't see it. But it is taking us all ahead from past to the future."

He quickly took out a page from his diary lying on the table and drew an airplane.

"Wooooow. Such a big airplane." Her eyes opened wide, and she got up in excitement clasping her hands. Even Pedro's eyes went wide looking at her excitement.

"So, who is driving this airplane, Grandpa?" And that was enough to bring down his excitement. He continued with the analogy that he had started, "You see Maria, time is driving the airplane all by itself."

"Wow. It must be very powerful and smart, isn't it?" Her eyes went wide again, she almost started jumping on the table. He too got thrilled. It was almost like mirroring her. And then came the next one, "So when did this airplane start?"

This was the last straw breaking Pedro's capacity to think any further.

His stumbling thoughts and her question parade were interrupted by the shrill tone of the phone ringing. Pedro exclaimed, '*Saved by the bell*,' under his breath and ran to pick up the phone. It was his old friend, Stuart.

"Thank you for calling, Stuart. This means a lot to me." Pedro took the phone and walked a little further away from the table.

"Seems I saved you from a situation?" Stuart started laughing aloud.

"Hmmm. So, did you get my work done?" Pedro responded, changing the topic.

"I have collected *Eternity* from the big guy."

"Finally!" He gave a sigh of relief hearing the news as if he had just been waiting for it. "Could he solve it? He has already taken more time than he promised."

"I don't know about that." Stuart sounded clueless. "But he has given me a sealed letter for you."

"A letter? Sealed? That's strange!"

"Even I found it strange. But, when I asked him about the letter, he didn't utter a word."

"I just hope he has solved it. That's what matters. I

need to see that letter. Are you home?"

"I should be there in some time, say around an hour."

"I will come over."

Pedro kept staring at the phone as he hung up.

The big guy, Edward Quattrochi! Pedro's arch-rival for the last forty years. The young blood who came blazing into the industry and shook Pedro's sovereignty. With a design style exactly the opposite from that of Pedro, Edward had created a huge uproar amongst Pedro's patrons. Edward was sharp. He too, like Pedro, communicated through his designs; things that an ordinary eye would never notice. Pedro's style had the flavor of heritage, history and a sprinkling of mythology; Edward had a bent towards the modern and abstract. Although both had styles which were poles apart, they were both equally respected in the industry and continued to endure in the business

Forty years and they had never seen eye to eye about anything or even exchanged words beyond mere social necessities. Their egos had done the talking most of the time. Much of it created and savored by the people around them. They were carrying an unaddressed hatred for each other all these years. Both waiting for the other to blink first.

After all these years, Pedro did blink first. It was the last road he wanted to take, but it was the only one left. Pedro had knocked all possible doors of experts to whom he could trust his little secret mystery, but none of them could take him forward. He was growing old, losing on time. He had finally dared to share his secret with Edward. He was his last hope.

"Grandpa?" Are you alright?" Maria moved towards him and pulled his hand. Maria had been waiting there all this while for his call to get over. Her query was still unresolved, her story incomplete.

"Yes, Maria." He answered softly as he leaned towards her. He could see the concern in the little girl's eyes. But, at the moment he did not have any inclination or the right energy to address it.

"We need to go to Uncle Stuart's place." His playful tone had disappeared.

"Grandpa!" She made her distress quite apparent with a terse response. His change in tone and the sudden brake on her interesting airplane story hadn't gone too well with her.

This eight-year-old wasn't an easy cookie. But Pedro too wasn't any less. He forced a faint smile, "Don't you remember Uncle Stuart? We had gone to his park inauguration a year ago. You played there the entire evening."

Her eyes lit up again, "Yes. That new park. I know. That's a nice place." The mood changer had worked.

"We will go to the park first and then to Uncle Stuart's house. Both are just next to each other."

Vivid memories of the games at the park had put a halt to time and the airplane. Pedro was too preoccupied after his conversation with Stuart. Even for him, at that moment, time and airplane were of lesser concern. He had bigger complications to deal with.

Stuart's house was half an hour away from Pedro's place. He comforted Maria in the backseat of his car and hit the road immediately. He switched on the radio and increased the volume to sidetrack any conversation with Maria.

Pedro's thoughts took him to the biggest unresolved mystery in all his years on earth. A mystery that had defined his purpose in life.

Stuart was one of Pedro's oldest friends, and both of them had graduated from the same college. While Stuart had taken charge of his family business, Pedro had joined the designing team of a watch manufacturer.

Over the years, Pedro had created a mark in the watch industry while Stuart had turned into a philanthropist after retiring from his family business. Pedro considered him as his closest friend and confided in him the most.

It was a lazy afternoon and there were hardly any vehicles on the road. They didn't take too long to reach the park.

Stuart had always dreamt of creating a park for children. A place where they could play all day without anyone bothering them. After handing over the business to his son, he fulfilled this dream.

Pedro parked the car across the street and held Maria's hand as they crossed the road. The park seemed reasonably calm for a Sunday. When they reached closer to the gate, they were astonished at what they saw. It was locked. The rusty lock and clinging shrubs on the gate were a clear indication that the park had been non-functional for quite a while.

"That's strange," remarked Pedro, turning to Maria who seemed upset on seeing the closed gate. "I think we need to check with Uncle Stuart."

Stuart's place was just a block away from the park. Pedro and Maria decided to walk to his house. Stuart lived in his ancestral mansion, which was more than a hundred years old. The old structure distinctly stood out amongst the modern-day constructions in the street.

Pedro rang the bell as they stood outside the main door. "Pedro. Good to see you!" Stuart greeted Pedro as he opened the door. "Oh! Hello young lady," he added on noticing that Pedro had company. Pedro and Maria followed him to the seating area.

Before they could even sit down, Stuart picked up a black watch box and a sealed letter, from the table and handed them to Pedro. "Here's your letter and here's your *Eternity.*"

He kept staring at the letter in Stuart's hands, his

eyes filled with hope. He finally took it but stood there vacillating, whether to open it or not.

"Thank you Stuart. I..I..I." Pedro fell short of words to express his gratitude.

"Pedro. Better not bring all these 'Thank-Yous' between us. Just open the letter and see if Edward has got it right. Does it answer the puzzle?"

From the moment his eyes fell upon the letter, Pedro had forgotten that Maria too was with him. However, Maria was least upset. She had made herself comfortable in a recliner chair in the corner, and was busy staring at the huge chandelier hanging in the middle of the room.

Stuart helped Pedro open the sealed letter. Pedro slowly opened it, his heartbeat racing high and still skeptical of the matter it contained. He read through it in no time. He turned the page to check if there was anything written at the back. He certainly did not look pleased with the response.

"Two months and this is what he gives me! A negative response?" He said with a lot of angst.

"Calm down Pedro. Calm down. What has he mentioned?"

Pedro handed over the letter to Stuart. Stuart started reading it aloud.

"Hello Pedro!

I am sure you were waiting to hear from me. Apologies for taking so long. The subject shared by you is truly unique. I have never seen, heard or read about anything like this. I am amazed that such a watch exists in reality. Apart from its uniqueness, there is nothing very peculiar about the watch that could help me make a possible headway in my search. Not even a tiny symbol etched on it. I have explored all possible texts to check for any reference to its rare trait, but not even a single word about such a phenomenon has been mentioned anywhere. I went into a lot of technical detail as well, to decipher the system behind it, but the mechanism of the watch is too simple to have any room for such possibilities. Even mathematically there is no rationale for it.

I am writing this letter with a lot of regrets as I couldn't be of any help in your pursuit. Regards, Edward Quattrochi.

P.S. You are probably focusing in the wrong direction. The answer may not lie in the watch. It may very well be between the inside and outside."

"At least he put an honest effort, Pedro. You have been with the watch for all these years and you couldn't discover a single aspect. Now you are expecting him to get it right in two months?"

"I am not angry, Stuart. I am disappointed. Grossly disappointed. Not with him, but with my own luck."

The feeling of ineptness was slowly creeping in. Pedro's eyes had become moist. Stuart stood there helpless, watching his friend breaking down. He went closer and patted his shoulder. He tried diverting his attention by attempting a discussion, "Pedro, what did he mean by 'between inside and outside'?"

"It's just some philosophical banter, I suppose." Pedro was clearly not interested in any conversation.

"I believe it's worth a consideration. You have been looking for a logical answer. Probably, it's time you look beyond the watch. *'Outside and in between'* whatever Edward was referring to." Stuart held on to his point of view.

Pedro raised his head and stared at him. He heaved a sigh. "Probably."

He suddenly noticed that the recliner chair was empty. 'Maria?' He glanced around the room and she wasn't there.

"Maria?!" He shouted, his voice full of panic.

"Relax." Stuart interrupted. "She went into the other room when you were going through the letter. Supposedly exploring the artifacts there."

And then, she entered the room running at his call.

"Yes Grandpa."

His eyes showed genuine concern for her.

He bent down and pulled her cheeks. "Where were you Maria?"

"I was just looking at the paintings in the other room. They are very huge." She came a little closer to him and whispered in his ears. "And they are a bit ugly too."

They both laughed.

She looked at Stuart. "Uncle why is the park closed today?"

Pedro added. "Oh yes, Stuart. It completely went off my mind too. Why is your park closed? What happened? You always wanted to make a place for kids to play and you put in all this time to get it done. Then, why on earth is it shut?"

"Long story, Pedro. Yes, you are right. I created it for the sole purpose of their enjoyment. That was my clear motive."

"Then why?"

"In the initial days of the park, the kids played nonstop for long hours. Didn't you also see the enthusiasm on the first day? They sat on all the rides and shared everything in the park. But gradually, the picture started changing. Their behaviours started showing a different colour. They formed groups, started defining boundaries. Not letting other kids play with rides in their boundary, like they owned those rides."

He paused, looked at Pedro and Maria and continued, "It's my park and I didn't want any such rules. I intervened a couple of times. And when they continued coming back to their groups, marking their territories, I shut the park. End of story."

It was definitely a tough call for him. The agony was quite visible. He wasn't too happy with the way events had turned out.

Pedro looked at him, not able to make any sense of

it. "But they are kids, that's the way they are Stuart, isn't it?"

Stuart responded staring at Pedro, "It starts right at this age, Pedro. You are talking about kids, have grownups ever understood that nothing belongs to them? They are just supposed to play their part and leave." Stuart sat back having made his point.

"Hmmm," Pedro sat back and went into deep thought, deliberating on Stuart's standpoint. Stuart had always been a strong advocate of moral values and was constantly upset with people's greed.

Maria was lost, unable to make anything of what Stuart spoke. Pedro got up to leave. He held Maria's hand and started walking towards the door. As he took a few steps ahead, he looked back at Stuart and said, "If nothing belongs to anyone, then I suppose, even the park doesn't belong to you. So, shouldn't you just open it?" He opened the door, smiling and winking at Stuart.

Stuart sat there speechless, not knowing what hit him, as Pedro and Maria stepped out.

Pedro was feeling lost with the response he had received from Edward. He had pinned all his hopes on him.

He came out of Stuart's house not knowing what to do next. He held on to Maria's hand and walked towards his car. Maria stopped him and pointed at a nearby ice cream parlour. He loved ice creams, but his professional image and stature had created barriers in letting him enjoy those little pleasures. With Maria around, he always used the chance to relish his desire under the garb of getting ice creams for her.

They crossed the road and entered the parlor. They took the latest flavors from the counter and sat in a corner.

Maria took one bite from the scoop and spilled some on her watch. Before she could even realize it, Pedro was at his task of picking up a tissue and cleaning it. He was glad to see it ticking accurately. "Grandpa, why do you like watches so much? Did your grandpa also gift you a watch?" Maria's series of questions started again, but these, thankfully, were in Pedro's favor. It was one of the defining moments of his life, which he cherished the most. He had shared it with only a few people.

"I will tell you if you promise to keep it a secret. Our little secret!"

His statement was enough to arouse her interest in his story even before he started narrating it. She nodded in agreement, all ready to listen to her Grandpa's secret tale. He too started with total enthusiasm, pushing his ice cream aside.

"When I was a kid, my dad took my mom and me to visit Stonehenge, the most mystical and mysterious place that I have ever seen. It was my longest journey back then. We stayed with one of dad's old friends, Uncle Joseph. He was kind enough to drive us from the city to Stonehenge.

His car gave signs of trouble right since we sat in it. We had our apprehensions, but Uncle Joseph was confident that it wouldn't break down. So, we continued. It was a long, uncomfortable drive through a narrow path on the plateau. Our plan was to reach a town named Amesbury by late evening, spend the night there, and visit Stonehenge early next morning.

It had already become dark before we crossed the

plateau. There was absolutely no sign of the moon in the sky and the evening was just growing darker. I had fallen asleep in mom's lap, dreaming. A dream so absurd, that I still remember it clearly.

I was running, gasping for breath in the dark. I felt I was being chased by an old man and I was trying to run away from him. We seemed to be running in a gigantic circle. I was running as fast as possible, trying to get away from him, but I could hear his footsteps catching up at the same speed. At one moment, although scared, I looked behind. And to my surprise he wasn't there. I instantly stopped and turned around. There was no one there, not a single soul in sight. Just a plain field lit up by stars. I was still very scared. I decided to head back wherever I was going. The moment I turned, he was standing right in front of me, giving me a cold stare. I screamed my lungs out, 'Mom! Help!' I woke up screaming.

The scream shook everyone in the car, especially Uncle Joseph. He lost his grip on the wheel and 'Thadam'! The car banged into a tree on the side of the road. We moved out of the car without making much noise and checked if everyone was alright. Luckily, none of us got any injuries. Except for the car!

Then all hell broke loose. For almost an hour, my dad and mom gave me a sound hearing.

I was feeling extremely terrible. For everything! For Uncle Joseph, his car, mom, dad and the entire mess.

It was pitch dark and the place looked completely deserted. Not many vehicles used to take that road. Even those few, who would take it, would travel only in daylight. The nearest town too was miles ahead. Uncle Joseph tried his best, but the car seemed to have given up.

After a lot of deliberation, we decided to spend the night in the car and search for help at daybreak. I was the first one to fall asleep while the others were catching up on old times.

I heard someone calling me. I opened my eyes. Everyone in the car was sleeping. I was very sure I heard some voice calling out my name. I looked outside the car. To my utter surprise, I could see Stonehenge across from the car, a little distance away. We hadn't even noticed that we were so close to it all this while. Fortunately, the stars had lit up the place.

I cannot forget the sight of those magnificent stones.

Just then, I heard some sound. It was coming from around the stones. It felt like the same voice that I had heard before. I woke up my mom and told her about it. Although sleepy, she tried checking for any strange sounds but couldn't hear any. She told me that it was probably just a voice in my own head. She asked me to go to sleep. I tried sleeping, but the sound continued. I kept looking at the huge stones as I lay in the car. They seemed to be inviting me. I had this urge to find out if someone was actually there, calling out for me. But I was very scared. Somehow, I gathered courage and opened the door. I slowly walked towards the massive structure. The sound was getting clearer as I moved closer to the Stones. It was quite a walk. I was scared, inquisitive and astounded all at the same time. It wasn't as close as it appeared from the car. The moment I reached there, the sound vanished. The place was dead silent. I waited there, confused, trying to hear at least some sound. But the wait seemed futile. Mom was probably right; the voice was running in my own head.

But the look of the stones was too alluring for me to return to the car. They were like little mountains, standing in an array, creating their own artistic spectacle. And on such a starry night they appeared even more stunning.

The stones gave a feeling of serenity and intimacy. I wasn't scared anymore. With the glittering, star-studded sky in the backdrop, it created an unparalleled visual spectacle. Gazing at the stars, I wondered what they did hanging up there. It almost felt like they were looking back at me and wondering the same. I introduced myself to them. They glittered even more when I spoke. It seemed they were interested in knowing about me. I started talking to the stars about myself, my dad, my mom, my school, about almost everything. And within no time, I stretched myself on the grass and fell asleep.

It was only at daybreak, when the first few rays of the sun hit our side of the earth, that I woke up. My eyes still closed, I could hear my dad shouting my name. I slowly opened my eyes, squinting at the sky searching for the stars, checking if they were still there or had hidden behind the sun.

I turned and waved to my dad, just giving him an assurance that I was alright. He looked at me and headed back to see if he could be of any help to Uncle Joseph, who had now opened the bonnet.

I looked at the stones surrounding me. They were massive. Much bigger than what they appeared in the night. My neck started aching as I gazed at their peak beaming in the sunlight. I looked down to hide my eyes from the glare of the sun. I saw my shadow, a pretty long one, touching the foot of one of the stones. It almost appeared like I was in the center of a massive clock and my shadow was showing the time. The mere thought that I was creating time baffled me. I was so ecstatic that I started jumping there screaming, '*I am time! I am time!*'

Just when I was in this all-encompassing euphoria, I noticed some movement behind one of the stones. I could feel someone standing there. I thought it was probably mom or maybe dad trying to hide from me. I turned towards the car. And to my surprise, they were still near the car with Uncle Joseph, waiting for some vehicle to stop by and offer help. I gulped nervously. My mind started running in all different directions. If they were all there, then who could have come in the open field without anyone's notice?

Before another thought could invade my mind, I saw a shadowy tall figure coming towards me from behind the stones. It was the old man from my previous night's dream. Running away from him in my dream was scary enough but looking at him appearing right in front of me from nowhere, left me petrified in fear. He walked up to me and placed a watch in my hand. The watch wasn't working. But the moment it touched me, the hands of the watch showed sparks of life. They started moving. The old man said, 'This is your time.'

'Pedro. Pedro.' My dad's voice brought a gush of blood in my veins. I turned towards him. He was on the road, waving at me. 'Come here,' he shouted. I wanted to run to him, but I was so frightened that my feet were not ready to move. Even my voice refused to help me. My heart started sinking. I glanced behind me to look at the old man one more time. But he wasn't there! I looked around in all possible directions. He was nowhere to be seen. He too had disappeared, just like the sound the previous night. Was it my imagination? I opened my fist to check the watch. The watch was still there.

I frantically ran to my dad who was waiting for me and asked him if he had seen anyone around. He responded in disagreement. It was an open field with no space for anyone to hide.

A wagon had stopped by and Uncle John was talking to the driver. He signaled my dad who lifted me and got into the wagon. The wagon driver was a local young man who gave us a ride to the nearby town.

That's how my life with watches started. And you know something Maria, I never told my dad about that watch." He glanced at Maria who looked spellbound. Pedro's little terrifying tale had left her in a state of disbelief.

Words rolled on her tongue, trying hard to make way out of her lips, "Why?" she asked him.

Pedro responded with a smile, "Actually, I was afraid. I had already been a nuisance, causing the accident, moving out of the car without informing anyone and spending my night outside, in the field. I didn't want to give him another reason to scold me. Moreover, I thought he would not even believe me. He would have either taken the watch from me or asked me to return it or probably yelled at me for picking up strange objects from the ground. So, I hid the watch in my pocket."

She nodded her head, being sympathetic with his decision. With that point, Pedro had just stepped on her curiosity.

"Do you still have the watch, Grandpa?"

"Of course. I do." Pedro replied.

He put the black watch box in front of her.

"Grandpa, this is not your watch. I saw Uncle Stuart give it to you." She commented raising her eyebrows, ready to discount the story told by her Grandpa.

"This is the same watch, Maria. I had given it to him for some work. And he just returned it to me."

He opened the box and carefully placed the watch in her hand. It was a modest round pocket watch. Although simple, it had an aristocratic appeal to it, especially because of the exclusive gold timepiece working smoothly in the beautifully hand etched dial. The cover had a plain antique look with a dotted infinity sign engraved in the center.

"It's just a simple watch Grandpa," she said, a little disheartened on not finding anything in the watch matching up to the level of the story that he had just narrated.

"Yes, it is. In fact, it is the simplest watch I have known till date. Yet, I have never been able to understand it."

She looked at the watch again, still unable to find anything unusual about it.

"What's there to understand in it, Grandpa? You have made better-looking watches than this one!"

"Maria, this is not an ordinary watch. It has a uniqueness which I have, till date, never seen in any other watch."

"Really? What is it?"

"It never stops! The motion of the hands of this watch is in its true sense, *eternal.*"

"Whoa!" Maria exclaimed almost jumping out of her seat. "Is that even possible, Grandpa?"

Pedro continued with a grin, as if expecting this question, "I too had similar beliefs. This intrigued me so much that I started studying watches. And so, began my journey into the world of watches. From then on, I have been trying to create a masterpiece which would never stop."

Maria raised her eyebrows, waiting for him to continue further.

"But I haven't yet been able to unravel the mystery of this watch. No battery, no solar cell nor anything extraordinary. But it still keeps ticking. I named it *Eternity!*"

"Eternity! That's an interesting name for a watch." Maria paused and tried checking the watch from all sides, also being cautious to handle it carefully. While she was doing so, she again continued with her barrage of questions, "So, did you ever see that old man again?"

"No, I haven't met him in reality. But he does run after me in my dreams," he looked at her and they both started laughing.

"Grandpa why do you have such dreams?" she asked. And then without waiting for an answer, she continued, "Last night, I was running in my dream. I suddenly fell down and woke up startled. I could feel everything in the dream, as if it was happening for real." She paused to check if any ice cream was left. Seeing an empty bowl, she continued, "Grandpa, where does the dream happen?"

"Umm...it happens in your mind, Maria." Pedro tried gathering his thoughts and articulating, "The brain takes up random moments from memory and projects them."

"But my dream was not random. It looked like a proper story."

"That's because our mind has a habit of joining the dots and creating meaning."

"Ohhh!" She gave a yes, but the confused look on her face was quite obvious.

"Wait. Let me explain it to you. Give me your flipbook."

"My flipbook?!" She opened her bag and handed the flipbook to him.

"Look here. If you look at each page individually, it is complete in itself. Let me fold one page. Now when you flip it, the story will still look complete. Your mind will fill up for the folded page."

"Yes. This is so amazing. I made a dream flipbook!" She excitedly exclaimed.

Seeing that he had been successful in shifting her focus, he thought of keeping her occupied to avoid further questions. "Oh, you are done with your ice cream! Let's visit the museum in the next block."

They had a good time at the museum before returning home. Maria was exhausted, but in no mood to sleep. He picked up the day's newspaper and sat on the couch. She pulled out an old photo album and lay down beside him. She started going through the pictures.

"Grandpa, your award picture! Look at Grandma smile. She looks so pretty." It was a picture of Pedro's felicitation when he had been honored with the title 'Maestro of Time' for his exemplary work in watch designs over the decades.

"Yes. She was very pretty indeed." He turned to get a glimpse of the picture. Her smile seemed like a fresh memory.

"And look at this picture." She pointed to the next one. It was a picture of Pedro and his wife together posing next to an airplane.

"This was our first airplane ride," Pedro replied.

"Oh, like time?"

"What?" Pedro couldn't get it.

"'Time is like a big airplane' didn't you tell me today?"

"Oh. Yes," he asserted, hoping she wouldn't open the topic again. But he was wrong. She closed the album and sat back.

"Grandpa, you didn't tell me, who started the airplane of Time?"

Pedro at first wished he could disappear somewhere. But then he thought of moving ahead with his airplane.

"You see, Maria. The airplane started all by itself. The engine fired with a big bang and the plane started moving. And before the engine started, everything was still, just like our game of statue. The one in which, when you say 'statue' everyone has to be still."

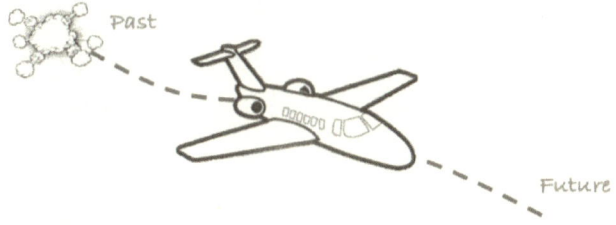

"The game of Statue, Wow!"

Pedro felt really happy at the simplified analogy that

he had created.

"Grandpa, who started the engine after the game?"

Pedro gave up, "I don't know Maria."

"But how can you not know? You are the Maestro of Time." She seemed to be in no mood to let it go.

Pedro had no energy to think further or carry on with explanations, "I don't know why I don't know, Maria."

He sat with his head in his hands, upset at the thought that Maria had provoked. "I never thought of inquiring into this space. No one ever asked me these questions. For that matter, even I have never asked myself such questions. Right now, I feel bewildered about my own knowledge on time." There was an underlying pain in his voice, as he made a comment on his own trifling level of awareness. Her questions, although simple, had left a big dent in his notions about time.

Maria, on realizing that he was upset, tried changing the topic.

"Grandma once told me, the only thing God gave us was time." She said with self-admiration, as if she had deciphered the mystery of time. Pedro acknowledged her effort with a cursory smile.

She slowly crept under his arms searching for a place on his lap to rest. And within a few moments she was fast asleep.

Pedro picked up the album and flipped through it. It had pictures from the early years of his marriage. Anna, his wife, had been his biggest support during those initial struggling years of business. He recollected his last moments with her.

"Pedro, get me time." She was breaking down from her long-drawn suffering of a malignant tumor. He had stood there, teary-eyed, holding her hand, helplessly looking at her. "You are the Maestro. You have a special connection with time. Do something Pedro, please do something." She lay on the hospital bed fighting with her destiny, begging for a miracle.

"I need my time." Her final words echoed in the hospital room before she took her last breath.

He had set time for the most complex watches and been a part of some of the most pathbreaking innovations in horology. But when it came to his love's last wish he had fallen short. He despised being referred to as the Maestro of Time, given that he had no control over time. He was merely ticking with time, just like everyone else.

Tears rolled down his eyes as the thoughts brought him back to the couch.

He then took out the picture of Stonehenge from the photo album. It was the picture of the day next to the old man incident. He had been terrified at the thought of going to the Stones again. He started questioning himself, *'Am I Time?' 'If not, then who is?' 'Who started the engine of this airplane?' 'Who is the watchmaker of this universal time?'* The old man had given Pedro the watch which never stopped. A watch that moved ahead with the universe. *'Was the old man the biggest watchmaker?'*

Maria was sleeping peacefully, but her innocent questions had infused an imbalance in Pedro's mind.

The old man was already chasing him in his dreams and now these questions too were after him. It was high time that he put the old man and the mystery of time to rest. He had to find out the answers.

Part Two

The Direction

*The mind will sow the doubt and
it will also show the way out.
Just flow.*

The next morning, Pedro got up early to prepare an elaborate brunch for his daughter, Sophie, who was coming to pick up Maria. He wanted to get the brunch ready before he took up the arduous task of getting Maria ready.

The moment Sophie put her foot in the house, she and Pedro caught up on updates in each other's lives. Sophie noticed the dark circles under his eyes, "You haven't been sleeping, dad?"

"Some questions keep you awake." He smiled casually as he responded.

"I hope it wasn't Maria and her endless set of questions." She glanced at Maria who was busy watching cartoons on the television.

"Questions more often bother us not because of their inquiring nature but because of our inability to provide the right answers." He looked at Maria, "Inquisitiveness is an essential ingredient for growth.

I see her becoming a renowned lady one day."

"Like you, the Maestro of Time." She grinned at him.

Pedro couldn't take it as a compliment anymore. He let the comment pass without any retort.

The brunch ended, but the conversation didn't. She asked him, "Do you remember the sage, Reishi?"

"Yes, of course. How can I forget him? He made one comment and, my revenues kept drifting down for almost a year. In fact, he has a place of worship in our town."

The picture of the unique circular design of the place of worship flashed in front of him. No walls, no doors, no windows and for that matter not even a deity. Only randomly placed white pillars. The placement of the pillars was such that from some places one would only see pillars and at the same time, there were some places from where one could see every nook and corner of that architecture. He had been quite mesmerized by the place of worship on his first visit. And more than the design, the 'no deity' element was the most enthralling aspect for him.

"The mesmeric Reishi. Yes. What about him?" he asked.

"He is coming to our town next month. Apparently, he has a massive following. Almost all my friends are lining up for his event."

"He does have quite a following, I must say." Pedro nodded in agreement.

"People also say that he is almost 200 years old," Sophie exclaimed in disbelief.

"People! People! They understand half of what he says and then make their own convenient interpretations."

"By the way, what was your fight with him about?" Sophie asked him, setting a pillow in her arms, eager to hear about the incident.

Pedro smiled looking at his daughter. "Ok. Ok. I will tell you. Maria is exactly like you, I must say."

He began narrating the incident. "Some of my friends, who believe in him, suggested that it would be good luck to receive his blessings for my then forthcoming watch. You know, I don't believe in such things. But then I saw no harm in presenting the watch to someone whose word could give an upward push to my watch sales. The idea was purely commercial for me. So, I did exactly as I was instructed. I went to the place of worship with my friends. We were there well on time to ensure that we got a place as close to Reishi as possible. Although people had come randomly, the seating was in such a way that an array of ripples got created encircling the meditating sage. In no time, the place was flooded with people. Most of them could hardly see him, but the mere thought that they were close to him, was probably fulfilling for them. We were seated on the second rung, very close to him. One of the visitors asked, "Why are there no walls, no doors at this place of worship?' And Reishi's response was as complex as his place of worship. He said, *'There is nothing to hide, nothing to protect here. Walls create barriers from self unto others and unto nature. What if you were never supposed to enter or leave, then would you create the door in the first place?'* The answer was no doubt brilliant. Everyone seated over there was in awe. Although I doubt if they understood what he actually meant. I raised my hand. He glanced at me but gave a chance to someone else. "Why are there no deities in this place of worship?" And there came another profound thought, *"In front of whichever God you believe in, what do you do? You close your eyes and ask for things that will give you acceptance, don't you? You give your prayers or offerings in the pretext of acceptance, don't you? Worship, in its true sense, happens when you become true to yourself. No facades. No masks. Just the true you. Naked. Real. Accepting yourself truly and completely is worship. The only thing you need for worship is you.*" After this answer, most of the crowd felt that their questions were irrelevant, and they withdrew their hands. I too was immensely impressed with his philosophy. Money and fame seemed utterly materialistic elements and complete misfits in this spiritual forum. I wasn't keen on raising my hand anymore. However, my friends were on a different page. They pulled my hand up and spoke for me. "Master, our friend Pedro is a renowned watch designer. He has come all this way to gift you one of his latest designs." It was an embarrassing moment, although, since they had said it, I stood up to present the newly designed watch. Even without looking at the watch he commented, '*Watches are insignificant.*' He declined my gift. That was the last I saw of him. Reishi's word became a force against my brand. His word spread fast. And his followers, without understanding the relevance of his remark, just boycotted my watches. Even the stores started withdrawing my series."

"How could he say this to you? You are the 'Maestro of Time', dad. How can someone challenge you on watches and time?" Sophie asked, looking a little agitated at what seemed like a loose comment. Then thinking about it, she asked, "But what did he mean when he said, 'Watches are insignificant'?"

"Even I don't know. I wanted to ask him. But I didn't get a chance. He went ahead with other questions, then meditation, then a talk on the topic of the day. I waited till the end, but he was swarmed with people. My friends were reluctant to let me question their Master, so they pulled me out of that place," he shrugged his shoulders. "Later I was too busy managing my dropping revenues."

Sophie excused herself as Maria called for her.

By then Pedro's thoughts had wandered back to the place of worship. He could vividly see the Reishi seated there, saying, '*Watches are insignificant.*' Were his remarks pertinent to Pedro's present pursuit? Reishi was a distinguished individual. Maybe he would be able to throw some light in the direction of Pedro's foray.' Pedro smiled as a mere discussion in a completely different realm had opened doors to a fresh path.

The moment Sophie and Maria left, Pedro knew just what he had to do. He got into his car and headed to Reishi's place of worship.

It was noon and Pedro wasn't sure if it was an appropriate time to go there. He wasn't even aware of visit timings… even if there was something like that. At this moment, the only thing that was on his mind was 'Time', and nothing else mattered.

The place was relatively empty. Only a few people were seated there, meditating. There was some kind of stillness in this place, which could not go unnoticed. Pedro went around the place looking for him.

The place was simple in the way it was designed yet difficult to understand. Pedro recollected his visit to the place with his friends. He was as confused then. And when he commented on the chaotic design, his friends had shared their interpretations on the design. One of them was of the view that the pillars just existed and there was no meaning to their placement. Whether one saw them as barriers or path makers was a mere reflection of the viewer's outlook towards life. For another friend the pillars never existed; whenever he had come over there to see the Master, he would only see him and not the pillars.

Pedro was walking across the place of worship with thoughts laden in his mind about the pillars and his friends. He seemed to come back to the same place from where he started. He couldn't find the sage anywhere in the entire premise. He first thought of asking for help, but then didn't think it wise to disturb anyone. He stepped out of the place and decided to try his luck the next day.

That night Pedro researched different perspectives of time. But he got further perplexed with the scientific theories. Even the literature of different religious texts did not provide any clarity. All had but one thing in common, time was endless.

Early next morning, he left for the place of worship. He was contemplating about the various theories he had read the previous night and about the genesis of time. Engrossed in his thoughts, he didn't realize that he had reached there. He walked in without hesitation, still in a daze. This time around the pillars had gone unnoticed and he had walked straight into the sage. It was when he saw him that Pedro became aware that he had already reached his destination. He smiled to himself trying to figure out how he made it this time. He looked at Reishi who was lost in meditation. Pedro sat in front of him at a little distance watching him.

Peace and calmness reflected on his entire frame. He looked tough yet approachable, someone with whom you could share your darkest secrets, someone in front of whom you would want to be the real you.

Moments later, Resihi opened his eyes.

"What brings you here, oh master of watches?" he asked noticing Pedro in front of him. Pedro was taken aback at his astounding recall. Reishi had remembered him, even though he had seen him only once before.

"I am sorry to have come so early and that too without a prior appointment. I came here yesterday also but ended up wasting half an hour in this bewildering place, searching for you."

"How can you waste something that does not belong to you?" came an odd query from Reishi.

"What? I am talking about time time that belongs to me," Pedro made an attempt to clarify his remark.

"Are you saying that time belongs to you? That's very good." Reishi commented with a straight face while mocking Pedro with his words.

"Excuse me! I didn't say that. I only said my time." Pedro was getting agitated with Reishi's sardonic style.

"Are you saying, each one has a share of time, which is their own time?"

"No. See, I have a life of say 100 hours from the time of my birth to the time of my death. Doesn't that belong to me?" Pedro simplified, just as he would have explained to Maria.

"If you say so," he responded with a sly grin leaving it open for Pedro's interpretation.

"When I say it belongs to me, I mean...you know what. Forget it!" said Pedro almost giving up the conversation.

Reishi was smiling as if enjoying the torment that Pedro was going through. He asked, "You said you were searching for me. Tell me, how can I be of any help to you?"

Pedro was still holding onto the previous conversation trying to make sense of it. Reishi looked at Pedro, deep into his eyes, as if trying to take a glimpse into his mind and catch his train of thoughts. Pedro was still lost.

Reishi moved his gaze to the river on the outskirts of the place of worship. "Watchmaker, what do you see there?" He asked Pedro pointing to the river.

Pedro's eyes followed the trail to where the finger was pointing. "A river," he answered, raising his eyebrows at such an obvious question. Pedro looked back at the sage. Reishi's eyes were still fixated on the river. He was seeking more than what he got as an answer from Pedro. Pedro, realizing this, looked back at the river to see what he had missed, this time being more observant.

"Calmness!" he exclaimed, immediately turning to the sage.

Reishi's eyes came back to Pedro, "Good," he said,

giving a faint nod. Pedro heaved a sigh of relief. It was the first question that he had answered acceptably.

Reishi tossed a small stone into the river creating ripples across the calm waters.

"What do you see now?" he asked again looking at the river.

"Ripples flowing one after the other." Pedro again tried articulating to suit the sage's expectation. "Disturbance," he almost shouted.

"Very good. One of the two states is what you seek." Reishi gave his perspective on Pedro's anguish. Reishi was no ordinary man. He was indeed a master in his own realm. But Pedro was still unclear.

"Disturbance and Calmness! One of them is time?" Pedro couldn't make any sense out of it. "Why do you always talk in riddles?"

"Pedro. Do you eat vegetables raw?" Pedro shook his head. Resihi continued, "Then why does the universe grow them raw? You would eat as per your taste, wouldn't you? And developing the raw food to suit your taste buds is your job, not the universe's responsibility. This is the simple, straight, raw language of the universe. And your interpretation lies with you."

"Master...but," Pedro unknowingly addressed him as his Master. In the span of a short conversation, his admiration for Reishi had gone up high and this slip made him further conscious of how Reishi would react.

Reishi noticed Pedro's unrest and handled it in his own charming way. "There is no Master and there is no disciple. The question that moves you into a state of disturbance is your master and only that will lead to your answer."

"But it was never my question."

"I threw the stone into the water. Where did the restlessness exist? In me or the water?"

Pedro looked at the water and continued the point Reishi had just made, "And the water would itself become calm. Becoming calm is only in its own control." He looked at Reishi who nodded in agreement.

"But what if I don't have the answers?" Pedro asked continuing with his apprehensions.

"The answers will keep coming to you in raw forms,

as your dreams. The interpretation only lies with you. You would get it when you would get it. Your question brought you to me. It would take you to your answer too. It is your only true Master."

"I can listen to you the entire day. But in the end, I don't know whether I am clearer or more confused."

"Confusion precedes calmness. Let it settle."

"According to you, calmness and disturbance are two words that define everything!"

"Is there anything else apart from the two?" he smiled, "When you get it you would get it."

"Doc, I have been having this recurring dream since I was around ten." Pedro hadn't been to a shrink all his life. But now it was different. He believed the answers were in his own mind and a little help could direct him to reach the right nerve where the answers were probably hiding.

"What is the dream?" the Doctor asked.

"It is pitch dark. I see this old man following me and we are running in a circle." He looked at the Doctor expecting an acknowledgement or an interpretation. The Doctor was quietly making notes. He just gave a slight nod waiting for Pedro to continue.

"Then I stop running and wake up scared. That's it." Pedro said shrugging his shoulders, making a point that there wasn't anything else to say.

"That's it? Is that all you remember of your dream?"

"Yes."

"Has anything changed in the dream over the years?"

"Nothing!" was his immediate response. Then suddenly he stood up with his hand on his forehead, "Wait! Wait! Wait! Wait!" as if discovering something new in his old dream. "There is a small change. I have grown over the years in the dream, but the old man hasn't. He is still the same."

"And he has never been able to catch you?"

"No. He is very far behind me. Almost diagonally opposite to my side of the circle."

"Hmmm. Interesting." And, the doctor continued, "Why do you feel he is trying to catch you?"

"I don't know why I feel that. What else could be the reason for running behind me?" Pedro said as a matter of fact as if there wasn't any other possible reason that he could gauge.

"Can you describe this old man for me?"

"He is dressed like you and me. Sophisticated. I can't see his face clearly. It is very blurred. But there is some calmness about his face. Although he seems to be running, he isn't tired or frustrated."

"Have you met anyone like him till date?"

"Yes. I have. He is very similar to an old man I met during my childhood, on a trip to Stonehenge. In fact, the dream started the same evening, just before I met him."

"In that dream, could you see him clearly?"

"I don't remember Doc."

"Do you remember the looks of the man you met at Stonehenge?"

"No Doc. But I feel it was the same person."

"Alright. What happened at Stonehenge? Was anything in your meeting unusual?"

Pedro grinned as he looked at the Doctor. "I don't know whether you would believe it or not. But the meeting was very unusual." He patiently described the entire incident of his Stonehenge visit. The Doctor was quite unmoved, unlike the other audiences that Pedro had shared the incident with.

"So, you still have the watch?"

"Yes. I do. And it is still working!" Pedro mentioned to make it clear to the Doctor that this was a miracle and not just some story in his head, like his other patients. He continued, "I am a watchmaker by passion and profession, but I have never seen a watch like this anywhere else. I have opened it several times, but there's not a clue on where it draws energy from!"

"Hmmm. I see. Very interesting story, I mean incident. And mysterious too. Just one more question. Why after almost 70 years are you curious to decode this dream?"

"Probably it has answers to something which is bothering me. And I am not able to figure that out," said Pedro, with a wry smile.

"I see."

"Let us do one thing now. I will put you in a relaxed state, which will slowly make you fall asleep. And let's see if you see this dream again. But this time, you keep running and do not stop. Is that clear?"

"Alright."

The moment the Doctor started the process, Pedro was asleep in a flash.

And within no time he was in his dreams. The old man also seemed to be waiting for him to fall asleep. Pedro ran, as if running for his life. The old man was behind him, pacing up. Pedro heard the Doctor's voice. 'Keep running.' He ran fast, faster than usual. He glanced behind to check for the old man. He was missing. And as he turned his sight again in front, he woke up shocked gasping for breath.

"What happened Pedro?" Doctor asked, handing over a glass of water to Pedro.

Pedro drank some water and rested for a while to get his breath back. "I ran faster than I normally do. Then, when I turned back to look at the old man, he was out of sight. But the moment I turned my head he was standing right in front of me."

"Interesting. Could you see the old man's face? Was

the person standing in front of you the same as the person running behind you?"

"It was the same person. But I couldn't see his face again. It was still blurred."

"Could you feel or gauge the old man's feelings? I mean whether he seems to be angry or..."

"He seemed quite relaxed when he was right in front of me. As a matter of fact, there was no aggression that I could feel."

"*Then why are you running?* Let me put it this way, '*what are you running away from?*'"

"I don't know Doc. I really don't know."

"Alright. Let's end this session here. We will meet again next week and continue our session."

"Doc, I may not be able to make it next week. I plan to travel to Stonehenge."

"That's good. Have you been there after that incident?

"No Doc. Never." Pedro shook his head.

"And may I know the reason why?"

"Fear. I have been too scared."

The childhood episode had clearly left a heavy impact on him.

"And what makes you go there now?"

"It's about time I faced my fears." Pedro shrugged, not emphasizing further.

The Doctor smiled in appreciation. "Good to know that. Then let's catch up when you return."

Pedro came out of the building and headed to the parking lot where he had kept his car. He looked at the building and realized that it was circular too. 'Why do all these circles come in my life?' He said to himself and moved ahead. Right then a man came from behind and before Pedro could even think, he snatched his pouch and ran. The pouch had all the documents required for his travel and his precious watch, *Eternity*. Pedro wouldn't let him run away with it at any cost. He ran with all his energy behind the man. The man was running around the building. Pedro just followed him not letting him go beyond his eyesight. A policeman stopped Pedro, "Excuse me. Please stop." He took him aside and asked, "Why is that man following you? What's going on?" Pedro was zapped at this allegation and more so at the misunderstanding. "Officer, I am following him and not the other way. Can't you see? Isn't it obvious? He has taken my pouch which has all my important documents."

"Oh. I am really sorry. From where I saw, I felt he was following you. Just wait over here. I will get your pouch." He made a quick call and gave the description of the thief and pouch. Within minutes one officer got him to the place where Pedro was waiting.

"Thank you, officer." He said as he took back his pouch to check if everything inside was intact.

"It's alright Sir. I am sorry for my misunderstanding. When people run in circles it is difficult to guess who is following whom."

Pedro sat in his car and as he put the key to start the car, his eyes shot up. The officer's words echoed in his mind, "When people run in circles, it is difficult to guess who is following whom."

'*Has the old man been following me or have I been following him?*' He recollected his dream. 'The moment I started to run faster, I lost him from behind me and there he was standing in front. *Has he even moved from his position all these years?*'

This was getting even more complicated then he thought.

He felt something wet on his knee. It had got bruised badly when he was running. In the frenzy, he hadn't realized that he had hit something and had started bleeding too. He went back to the hospital building to get a dressing on his wound.

"It isn't that bad." The physician told Pedro in a reassuring tone, calming him down. "It will get healed by itself in a few days. I will just bandage the wound and prescribe you some medicine. Take it from the chemist downstairs."

"Doc, how does it heal by itself? Does it mean my body doesn't need medicines?"

"The human body is an aggregation of various cells. These cells have the capability to regenerate and heal by themselves. The medicine I have prescribed is to ensure that the wound is protected during this healing process."

"So, our cells die during an injury or similar physical issues?"

"Yes, they do. And they die naturally too. And new cells are born. It is a continuous process."

"So then can I say that an individual is a completely new person after some time because all his old cells have died and have been replaced by new ones?"

The Doctor laughed at the thought presented by Pedro. "I have never really thought about it. Although, people are still researching on this perspective. But I suppose, in a way you can say that."

"But then how do I still remember things, when my brain cells would also be dying and being born again?"

"Some bit of memory gets stored at multiple places, not only your brain."

"That means the only thing which keeps moving

ahead is my memory, while I keep changing over a period of time?"

The Doctor's eyebrows were raised throughout the conversation at the amazing inferences Pedro was making. He could just say, "In a way you can say that."

"Thank you, doctor. Especially for simplifying it for me. I understand that there would be an entire science behind every word you speak. But you made it very easy and interesting."

He got out of the building, this time being extra careful about the pouch. He hadn't even left it in his car as he had some bad experiences in the past of things getting stolen from his car.

He thought of Maria as he started his car. He could feel the same inquisitiveness evolving in him. She had taught him one thing for sure, 'question the obvious.'

He reached his travel agent's office, which was only

a few blocks away. The bookings were full for the month. The only flights available were from Sophie's town, which was at a distance of five hours from his place. Pedro was fine with the extra travel, as it gave him an opportunity to meet Maria as well.

He started laughing on seeing his booking slip.

"What happened? Are the details in the slip alright?" the attendant asked.

"I can't believe it is the same date," Pedro responded.

"What date?"

"I travelled to Stonehenge around 70 years back. It was on the same date."

"Oh, what a coincidence!"

"There are no coincidences," he smiled. He collected his tickets and carefully placed them in his pouch as he left from there.

Stuart had offered to drive Pedro to the airport. They were to halt at Sophie's place for a quick snack before heading to the airport. Meeting Sophie and Maria were worth the exhausting drive.

On reaching their place, Stuart gave Maria a pack of chocolate cookies.

"These are for pushing your Grandpa to visit Stonehenge. You did something which I failed to accomplish in all these years."

Maria was busy unwrapping the cookie box, as Stuart shared the dilemma he went through while choosing between Chocolate cookies and Danish cream cookies at the store. She looked at him, "The next time you have difficulty choosing, get both the flavors for me." Pedro and Sophie burst out laughing.

Sophie had turned on the television to check the weather updates. Maria pulled out a cookie from the box and went to Pedro, who was all smiles. She placed a cookie in his hand and signaled him to come close. "If Uncle Stuart would have got Danish cream cookies our airplane would have headed in some other direction," she whispered softly in his ears and chuckled. Although almost inaudible, Pedro still heard her remark. He gave a surprised look at her, patting her head. He was taken aback by the brilliant parallels the little girl had drawn.

"Ok. Ok. Even we are here in the same room. What's with this gossiping?" Stuart commented looking at the two exchanging glances. "And where is my share of cookies?" he continued playfully.

"That's our little secret, Uncle," she handed him two cookies and ran into another room.

"What's this?" Sophie stood up panicking and increased the volume of the television. Two flights had crashed into commercial towers collapsing them to the ground. The death toll was going to be huge.

"This does not look good. Dad cancels your flights, immediately."

"What has happened is unbelievable. I understand that it is extremely painful. But, I am not cancelling my flights, Sophie. This has happened in some other place which has no correlation to where we are or where I am headed. If the flights are working, then I am not stopping." Pedro too was taken aback by the news. But his response had a reflection of a man who had made up his mind.

Sophie was almost in tears. "Uncle Stuart, please make him understand. Leaving at this moment can be fatal."

Pedro interrupted, "Sophie, my going today is extremely important. And trust me, nothing will happen to me."

Stuart added, "Let him go Sophie. I am going with him to the airport. And if things aren't fine over there, I promise, I will get him back."

Sophie started sobbing heavily. Pedro went ahead and hugged her trying to calm her down.

"Sophie, I will be fine. Don't you worry."

Stuart too came close to them and patted her back, "I know a couple of people at the airport. I will check with them when we reach the airport. You relax." He glanced at his watch. "I think we should leave now."

Sophie wiped her tears, "Dad, please take care of yourself."

Maria had just entered the room and was confused to see her mom and Grandpa teary-eyed. She felt they were just a bit emotional because of his trip. She walked up to Pedro and handed him her flipbook and a small pouch.

"This pouch has four stones gifted to me by Grandma. She said they bring good luck. I hope you meet the old guy."

Pedro took the stones and the flipbook and thanked her.

"I don't know whether I can meet him again. You see, he would be very old now. And people don't live that long."

"But he has magic. He gave you the magic watch. I am sure you will meet him."

He smiled at her innocent imagination. He didn't exactly know what he was going there for. Neither was he sure whether he would get anything there. But it just seemed the only thing he wished to do with his life at that moment.

He bade them goodbye and left for the airport with Stuart.

There was chaos across the entire airport. The news of the crashing flights had led to panic and fear amongst the travelers.

Pedro and Stuart headed to the counter to check if flights were cancelled. The counters were filled with travelers seeking information, with most of them resorting to cancelling their tickets. The Staff at all the counters were giving the same statements, 'Flights are delayed for at least 4 to 5 hours. Please wait for any further announcements.'

Stuart asked Pedro to wait there while he reached out to his friend at the airport office and checked the flight status.

Pedro stood in the queue at the counter as Stuart disappeared through the crowd.

Pedro had reached the counter, but Stuart was still nowhere in sight. He moved ahead and took the boarding pass. The moment he moved from the counter, Stuart ran in.

"Pedro, the security has gone tenfold high. They are checking everything multiple times before giving a go-ahead to any flight. Even an iota of doubt and they will cancel the flight. My friend suggests you push your travel by a day."

"Stuart, I am flying today. I have been fearing and running away my whole life. I have taken a lot of time to reach here. I can't stop now. Not even for a day."

"Pedro, you have waited all this while, a day won't make a difference."

"Stuart, time is testing my decision. Let me go with the flow."

Pedro had made up his mind. He was in no way taking a step back. Stuart tried all he could to make him change his mind, but finally gave in to his perseverance. Stuart wished him luck and requested him to call once he landed.

Pedro entered into a bookstore in the airport and picked up a newspaper. The entire waiting area was abuzz. There was hardly any place to sit. He located one lounge seat in the far corner and managed to reach there before anyone else could. He made himself comfortable and placed his luggage beside the seat. He thought of reading the newspaper but was feeling too sleepy because of the early morning drive. At the same time, he was too anxious about missing the flight by falling asleep. The display board showed the departure time after three hours. He got up, tore a page from his diary, wrote his name and the flight number in big bold letters and pasted it into his bag.

A gentleman sitting on the adjacent seat watched Pedro do his calligraphy. He called out to Pedro, "Don't worry," glancing at the page on the bag, "Pedro?" looked at him reconfirming if he got the name right. Pedro nodded and put his hand forward, so as to ask his name. They shook hands. "I am Prof. Philip Connery," the gentleman introduced himself. "My daughter and I are on the same flight. I shall wake you when there is any announcement."

"That would be very kind of you, Sir," Pedro thanked him. He lay down on the chair and closed his eyes trying to get some rest.

"Dad, isn't that the symbol of infinity?" Pedro could hear the voice of the Professor's daughter. Her voice reminded him of Maria.

"Yes, my girl. That is infinity. Do you know what infinity is all about?"

"Yes. Something that has no end."

The chat was turning interesting. Pedro, keeping his eyes closed, further eavesdropped on the conversation.

"You are partly right." The Professor replied. "Draw the sign of infinity and write down the numbers from 1 to 9. The answer lies in the way each number is represented."

His daughter drew the symbol and the 9 numbers on a piece of paper. Pedro also created the same in a line in his mind.

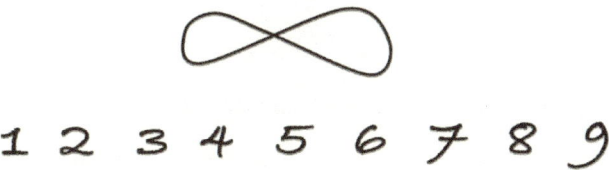

"Now tell me what is one thing that you find different in the 9 numbers and the sign of infinity."

"I don't see any difference," replied his daughter.

The answer resonated with Pedro's thoughts. There was no visible difference. Except that the number 8 was a vertical representation of the infinity sign. He wanted to answer but held himself back and continued listening to what the Professor had to say.

"Aren't all these numbers a representation of

something finite?"

"Yes," the girl replied.

"Then look at 8, which is a vertical representation of the infinity sign. That means there is something finite about infinity as well."

"I am sorry dad, I didn't understand." The girl responded with confusion written all over her face. Even Pedro couldn't get a grasp on what the Professor was trying to say.

"Ok. Look at these numbers carefully. Each number except 8 has a definite starting and an end in the way they are represented. Do you see it?"

"Yes, I do." The girl responded with an instant gleam in her eyes, as she could make sense of her Dad's perspective this time.

The Professor continued, "Now check if you can see that in the sign of infinity."

"There isn't any."

"They exist but are not visible. The end merges with the beginning and it gets into a loop giving an illusion that nothing ever started, and nothing ever ended."

"Oh yes!" the girl was delighted on getting it.

The Professor continued, "This infinity sign is depicted in ancient Egyptian and Greek scriptures in the form of Ouroboros, a dragon eating its own tail. It symbolizes the eternal cycle of renewal, creation out of destruction!"

Pedro stood up from his seat, looking shocked at the Professor and shouted, "That mean's time is finite."

He leapt up, took his bag and started running. He didn't know why he was running or where he was running to. It was like a eureka moment for him. He spotted a phone booth and stopped. He thought of calling up Maria. But then started contemplating. She was too young to even get the context, he thought. But he had to share it with her, so he still went ahead and made the call.

"Maria!"

"Grandpa!" She was all excited hearing his voice. "You reached?"

"No Maria, the flight is delayed."

"Oh. Ok. I thought …."

"Maria, I found out about who started the engine."

"Who?"

"It was '*No one*'." He was ecstatic and overjoyed to share his new findings.

"What? No one? Grandpa are you alright?"

"Maria. The airplane will eventually slowly lead to a big bang. This big bang would then start the time again from the beginning."

"Not able to understand a thing, Grandpa."

"Remember, I gave you a paper with the airplane drawing. Pull it out."

She did that and came back on the phone.

"Yes, Grandpa."

"Join the line from the future to the big bang in the past."

She did as was told, slowly sketching the dotted line."

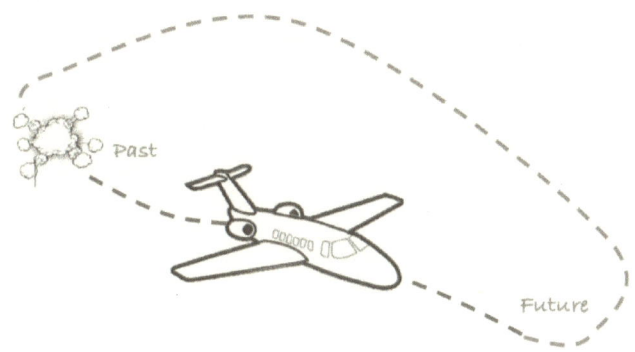

"Yes Grandpa, it's done."

"Now, what do you see Maria?"

"The airplane is headed to the future which is then headed back to the big bang which leads to the past and back to the same place."

"Perfectly right, Maria. Do you see that now? This is how time always started and this is how it would end. At the same point."

"Wow. This is great. You are awesome Grandpa. Truly the Maestro of Time."

"I will hang up the phone now. Do tell Sophie that everything is alright here and I will be boarding my flight in a couple of hours."

She said good-bye and hung up the phone. She could

hardly make any sense of what her Grandpa was trying to say. But she was excited that her Grandpa was very happy. The four stones of good luck had done the magic, she said to herself.

The boarding was finally announced. The delay had changed his entire schedule. He got into the flight and took his seat. Waiting for the flight to take off, he pulled out his diary and made the sign of infinity.

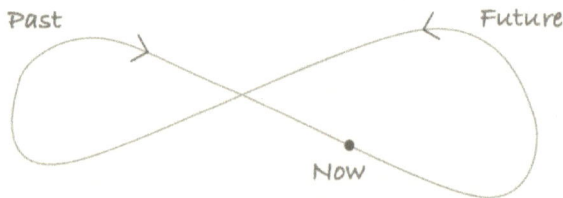

Amazed at the thought, he started making a note. *'While we believed, we were moving towards the future, we were actually moving towards our past. Time is like a big continuum that we are in.'*

The flight had just taken off. He pulled out his pocket watch. He kept looking at the infinity sign on it. Flashbacks of the old man handing over the watch to him were going on in his mind. The old man had pointed to the watch and told him, 'This is your time.' 'Was he trying to tell me the real essence of time? The sign of infinity was always here on the watch. Does it have any significance to what I am seeking? Will I get my answers at Stonehenge?' His thoughts were just not ready to stop. He opened the cover and glanced at the time. He kept looking at the watch. Something else had caught his attention.

He took his diary and drew the circular dial of the watch just below the infinity sign.

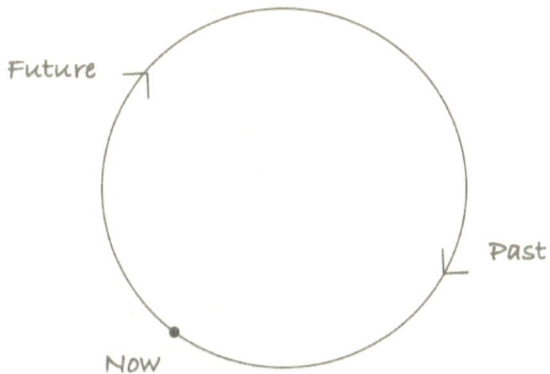

It resembled a Zero. Pedro noted the Past, Now and Future points on the Zero he had drawn. The same logic of infinity applied here too.

The Professor's words kept ringing in his ears. *'There was no beginning and there was no end. The end merged with the beginning and it got into a loop giving an illusion that nothing ever starts, and nothing ever ends.'* He looked at his watch. Even the watch showed exactly what the Professor had just said. He smiled looking at the sign of infinity on the cover and the dial inside.

He started making a note in his diary.

'Zero was the alternate side of infinity.'

'Time had always been finite. The end leads to the beginning.'

It was always right in front of him in his watch, but he could never see it. He kept smiling looking at his watch.

As he kept his diary in his pouch, his fingers touched the four stones, which were lying in his pouch. He pulled them out of his pouch, and carefully placed them on his left palm. Maria was right. They definitely had brought him good luck.

He closed his fist with the stones in it. Then opened it, removed the stones from his palm and smiled.

He recalled an old game his wife Anna used to play with Sophie when she was a kid.

"Hold these four stones in your hand and close your fist," she would ask Sophie. And Sophie would nicely oblige. "Now open your palm. What do you have in your palm?" she would ask.

"Only four stones," would come to an instant response.

"Now remove these stones. And what do you have in your palm now?" she would ask again.

"Nothing," again an instant and realistic reply from Sophie.

Anna would then say, "If you look at it, right now you have the entire universe resting in your palm. Isn't it?" And Sophie's eyes would light up.

Just the memory of the game and Anna brought a smile to his face.

But, it was only now after so many years, that he could understand its true meaning. Nothingness and everything were two sides of the same coin. Zero was the alternate side of infinity.

Just then the air hostess came and asked something. He was so lost in his thoughts that without even listening to her, he replied, "Nothing." Realizing this he instantly asked her apologetically to reiterate. She politely responded that she was checking if he was interested in eating something. Earnestly listening this time, he smiled and answered, "Nothing." To which she smilingly replied, "Everything is very good Sir, why don't you pick something up?" He laughed at her words. "I ask for nothing and everything is available to me. No thank you, ma'am. I am fine." He couldn't contain his laughter. Serendipity had got into action, he thought to himself, just as Reishi had mentioned.

The air hostess had gone ahead asking the other passengers. A kid on the seat behind him shouted in excitement, "Cookies!"

Pedro's eyes opened wide. He said to himself, 'Danish cream cookies, chocolate cookies.'

He slapped his forehead. 'Choices! Possibility of different futures! The permutations of the entire world and the choices each one makes at every moment. All probable paths finally converging to the big bang? The infinite path being a finite loop was impossible. Just impossible!'

The airplane from Pedro's page was now in turbulence. Ouroboros, the mythological serpent, had let go of its tail now. And the heads of the serpent had increased in number, each wanting to go a different path.

Pedro's euphoria had fizzled out. He just sat there waiting for the ride to get over.

Part Three
The Completion

If you end where you began,
Did you even move in the first place?

It had become pretty dark by the time the flight landed. Pedro's schedule had gone out of hand because of the flight delay. Stuart had booked a car for his pick up from the airport, while Pedro had made reservations for a room in the Amesbury guesthouse. The guesthouse was a long drive from the airport. He had made all arrangements in advance to avoid any travel in the night. But one delay and his plan had come crashing down like a domino. He was delayed, for the first time in his life. Being on time was Pedro's philosophy of life. Time was the basic essence and being on time every time was the only way he had known to live. People in his town and office used to adjust their watches looking at his daily activities. They used to also say, 'the watches may not be on time for once, but Pedro would always be on time.'

He got out of the airport and met his chauffeur who was waiting for him.

"Good evening, Sir. I am Joseph."

"Joseph!?" Pedro exclaimed.

"Does the name remind you of someone, Sir?" he asked as they walked to the parking lot.

"Yes. It does. And strangely he was the one who first drove me to Stonehenge."

"Ohh! I hope you had a good ride."

"Yes, of course. And quite a memorable one."

As they sat in the car, Joseph commented. "Sir, we are a little delayed from our schedule."

"Yes. I am aware, Joseph. I will pay the waiting charges. You know the whole episode of planes crashing into buildings that happened today. It had a domino effect on my plan."

"Yeah, I understand Sir." He smiled to himself, for getting the desired acknowledgement. "You won't believe sir, I was just watching the news and they were referring to a few people who had predicted many years before, about such an event happening."

"Oh, is it? Do you believe in such things? I mean, prophecies."

"Yes, I do, Sir. Some people have such powers. My mom has this habit of smelling something untoward happening much before it has happened. Like, she asked me not to go out today, for fear of some accident."

"Hahahaha… Do you believe her?"

"Yes, I do, Sir. She has never been wrong." The sternness in his response made it clear that he wasn't ok with someone laughing at his beliefs or at his mom.

"I am Sorry Joseph. I didn't mean to…I mean…you understand? I am sorry. By the way, how come you are out then?"

"It's alright, Sir. Actually, there hasn't been too much work lately. And I need to feed the family too, Sir. I had to come to work. And this road, I have travelled so many times since…"

Joseph kept on with this story, while Pedro's mind had already drifted. Different thoughts had started playing around in his head.

'Some people can see future events. Then either the event has already occurred somewhere, or it already exists somewhere at the same very moment.' 'Was the future pre-defined? Was destiny already decided?'

He pulled out his book.

'*If I was destined to reach a place, then did my choices even matter?*'

The Ouroboros in the center swallowed the rest of the heads, and the singular head got back to moving towards its tail. *There was always only one head which was supposed to reach the tail. The rest were mere illusions.*

Joseph was still on his story trail which had now reached his brother, who was living in some other country, and apparently doing very good in life.

Pedro without realizing that Joseph was talking, interrupted, "How many roads go from here to the town where we are headed?"

"Just one, Sir."

A queer smile, Pedro's eyes twinkled.

And Joseph continued with the story of the road coming into existence a century ago and how his ancestors used to walk down all the way.

Pedro's eyes were getting heavy and within no time he had fallen fast asleep.

He started having flashes of his first trip to Stonehenge and the mysterious stories he had heard about the place. And the mysterious old man and the watch he had given Pedro. This time the old man seemed to be standing there and staring at him. Pedro had never been able to remember his face. Even now in his dream, the old man looked blurred. Suddenly the old man appeared beside his car and was staring at him from outside the car window. But his face still looked too hazy for recognition.

Pedro raised his hand and cleaned the window to check on him, to ask, 'who was he? where he had been all these years?' The moment he cleaned the window, he was startled to see that the old man was none other than Pedro himself.

Pedro woke up shouting his lungs out.

Joseph, the driver was startled hearing this sudden

shout and lost control of the car, banging it into a tree just beside the road. The car had come to a halt.

Joseph jumped out of his seat and pulled Pedro out. "Man, are you out of your mind? We both could have died! You don't have many years, but I do have plans to live a long life!"

Pedro looked at his watch. It was the exact same time and the exact same tree where he had been through an accident 70 years ago.

"How could this be? How could this happen?" he kept repeating to himself.

"This happened because I was carrying an old gentleman who yells in the middle of the drive deafening the hell out of his chauffeur."

"I am sorry son. Take this money." He pulled out some cash from his pouch and put it in Joseph's hand. Pedro commented, "But I am not responsible for this. This was supposed to happen. I was supposed to stop here. This was always my destination. I just never saw it."

He looked at the stone structures from there. There was no moon in sight. Although it was dark, the stones were still shining. They seemed to be inviting him. As he looked at the stones, he experienced the same anxiety he had felt seventy years ago at this place.

He turned to Joseph. "You won't understand. It's destiny." He started walking towards Stonehenge. "You start fixing the car. I will be back in some time."

"Sir, you are not supposed to enter that area without permission. It is restricted. Sir, please come back." Joseph tried stopping him, but his voice fell on deaf ears. He turned back to his car, "Should have stayed back home. Mom was right. Again!"

Pedro had come this far at this moment and going back was nowhere in his mind. He didn't even bother to look back. He was walking towards the stone structure as a man possessed.

The ground was clear. There was no one around for miles. 'Who would be giving me answers here?' He thought, looking around at the vacant landscape. Except for the driver still working on his car, there was no one around. It looked quite similar to his uncle and father working on the car seventy years back. It was a perfect déjà vu moment.

He sat there on the ground and like the previous time started gazing at the stars. He was too exhausted to keep his eyes open for long. He didn't even realize that in a few minutes he was lying on the ground. And within moments he had fallen asleep. The same flashes repeated. He could see the old man again staring at him from behind the stones. Although his face could not be seen clearly even now, there was some kind of serenity and calmness on him. He came closer to Pedro and shook him and said, "It's time you wake up."

Pedro woke up flustered from his dream, not able to mark a difference between his dream and reality. He looked around to check if anyone was around him. But it was pitch dark. He looked at his watch to check the time.

It had stopped!

He stood up in shock. His watch had never stopped in the last seventy years. He stood there perplexed. All his life, he kept wondering and waiting for the watch to stop just to believe that it was a regular watch, and now when it had actually stopped, he just couldn't believe it. He frantically tapped his watch to make it start working. The very thought that he had a dead watch in his hand and he couldn't do anything about it made him more miserable. And that too, the very watch around which his life's journey was etched. The watch had been the biggest mystery in his entire life. He had always been captivated by the enigma behind its immortality. But now, the stopping of the watch had almost pulled out the purpose of his existence.

He stood there holding his watch, helpless.

The night had become darker. The thought about not having any idea of the time was further annoying. He tapped the watch again and brought it very close to his eyes to check properly. The hands of the watch had frozen and the ticking sound too had stopped.

"Your watch is showing the time in its truest sense," said a voice from behind him.

"Noh," he almost cried out, "The hands have frozen. How can it show....," he paused, realizing that there was supposedly no one there. Then, whose voice was he responding to?

He turned around to check. He could barely see anything. It was one of the darkest nights he had encountered.

"Who is it?" He frantically ran around to see if he could find anyone. He sprinted to the road to check if it was the driver who had called him. On reaching the car, he found Joseph sleeping inside the car. He ran back to the stones. He couldn't see anyone there either.

He walked around the stones and reached the center. The spot where he had shouted seventy years back, 'I am time'. He couldn't forget that spot. He checked to see if the shadow again rose from his feet like the previous time.

But it was too dark. There was no shadow. He smiled, shaking his head at his childlike behavior. He lifted his hand to check his watch. The dial looked lonely without the hands in motion. It was as if time had come to a halt.

He looked at the stones around and then glanced at his feet. Last time his shadow resembled the hands of a watch showing time. Now in the darkness, the absence of the shadow again resembled the current state of his watch.

'What a coincidence! Or was it by design?' He thought, talking to himself.

The dial and the stones around looked alike.

He recollected what Reishi had mentioned.

Calmness!

The dial was the only element in the watch that resembled calmness. Unmoved, indifferent, and unaffected by all the other moving elements in the watch.

He had never focused on the dial anytime in his life. His work had always been dedicated towards ensuring the hands kept ticking, that the disturbance in the hands existed.

"Yes, it is. Calmness and Disturbance coexisted in every watch," he shouted in excitement.

'But then, only one signifies time. That's what Reishi had indicated. I think I am moving in the wrong direction,' he told himself, with his excitement withering away.

"You are in the right direction." He heard the voice again.

"Joseph, is it you?" He shouted looking towards his

car. He could hardly see the car. He was sure he had heard a distinct voice. He turned around to check if there was anyone he could spot this time.

His sight wandered towards the stones. For a moment, he froze. He saw someone sitting in place of one of the missing stones. He held his breath and moved closer to the figure. He was shocked to see the same old man seated there. He appeared almost similar to what he was 70 years back.

Pedro almost dropped down as he saw him there.

"Who are you?" he asked, trying to gather his senses. It was too dark for him to see his face clearly.

"You will know when you will know," came a response from the old man.

'Why do I get such people around me? First the sage Reishi, who spoke only in riddles, and now this guy,' Pedro was talking to himself. 'Was this person an acquaintance of Reishi?'

He had heard rumors about Reishi's age. And here in front of him was a man, who Pedro felt had never aged.

"Are you the same person, I met...?" Pedro tried

asking. But his statement was cut short by the old man, who seemed least interested in conversing about his identity.

"You were searching for time. You are on the right track."

Although the conversation was in the direction of Pedro's search, he found it rude to be cut off in the middle of his statement. This old man had been giving him sleepless nights, and now too he wasn't very welcoming. He felt like giving it back, but then there was something about this person, that stopped Pedro. It was the same mesmerizing aura as that of Reishi.

He chose to continue the discussion, just in the hope that he would get his answers. "What direction are you referring to? Time has always been referred in motion. I have always been working on keeping the Disturbance alive, the hands ticking. And there is this other part of the watch, the Dial, which is Calm and does not move. Disturbance and Calmness coexist. They both together refer time. So, what direction are you referring to?" Pedro reiterated, trying to make his point clear.

The old man responded, "Motion is always relative

to something static. If all things are simultaneously in motion, and if nothing is static, then are they actually in motion?"

Pedro thought for a moment, trying to grasp what the old man was trying to say. He tried decoding it but finally gave up, "Could you be a little clearer?"

"I will explain in your language. Your airplane of time!"

"How on earth do you know about the airplane?" he almost got up. "Who the hell are you?"

"Sit Pedro. As I said, you will know when you will know. Now can we continue?" the old man said calmly gesturing to him to sit down. Pedro sat back not knowing where the conversation was headed.

"So, we were referring to your airplane of time." The old man continued, "If everything is in the same airplane, moving at the same pace, then is it actually moving or is everything at the same place? Even if you want the airplane to move, it has to be against something static. So, then what is static, if everything already exists in the plane?"

Pedro raised his hand, as if asking for permission to state his interpretation, "So you are saying, if we are seated in a moving car, for each other we are static, we haven't moved. And if everything outside the car also moves at the same pace as the car, then have we actually moved? The answer is No. We haven't moved."

"You are perfectly right, Pedro."

"That means the airplane has never moved?" Pedro asked, trying to reconfirm what he had just said.

The old man smiled nodding his head.

Pedro closed his eyes, trying to internalize it. He could feel vibrations in his body, as was the feeling of slowly moving into a state of meditation. He spoke, sitting motionless with his eyes closed.

"Motion is just an illusion."

He just recalled what Reishi had referred to.

"That means if Disturbance is just an illusion, then the true essence of time is Calmness."

He was just adding up all the possible correlations he could make.

"*So, the Dial is the true representation of time and not the hands!*"

He slowly opened his eyes and looked at the stones around him and smiled.

"The Stone structure in the night, representing the Dial without the Hands is true time!"

The vibrations were getting deeper, as he could slowly sense more and more cells of his body in that state. He continued, "If everything is static, then where are the past and the future?"

"They all exist together in the Time Continuum. Static." The old man replied.

'Infinity is an assimilation of finite points,' Pedro recalled what the Professor had said. He could visualize the sign of infinity with small finite points distributed throughout.

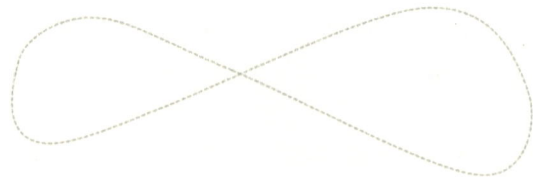

It was the symbol on his watch. It had been always there with him.

He removed the flipbook from his pouch.

"Each page individually is a reality and the story created through the flipping is just an illusion." He continued, "Every moment is complete in itself. So, you in the next moment is not exactly the same you."

"You are right Pedro. You are joining the dots perfectly. Getting a taste of the raw data presented to you," the old man smiled.

Pedro was now talking as he moved into an almost mesmerized state. "So, is anything moving? Why do we still have this feeling of moving ahead? Who is flipping the flip book?"

"The mind while moving from one static page to the other creates an illusion of movement. The same way you see in your flipbook. And you believe what you see. And then start seeing what you believe. So, then everything starts appearing in motion. And you start considering Disturbance, the moving hands of your watch, as reality," the old man replied.

"The mind is cruising through the flipbook. *The mind is the 'hands' of the watch taking me from one point of the dial to the other.*"

"If I am just a small part on each page of the flipbook,

then do I hold any significance at all? Am I even a watchmaker, to start with? Or am I a lost person? What am I? Or is my *being* limited to what the page demands?"

"You are none of these. And you are all of these." He took a pause, and then continued. "Pedro, you are each page of this flipbook."

"*I just am!*"

The vibrations had touched every cell of his body. He was in a deep state of Calmness. He slowly opened his eyes. He could see the old man's face clearly now.

The old man was none other than Pedro himself.

Pedro had reached a state where even this discovery was no longer disturbing to him. He had been running away, terrified, from the old man all his life. But on knowing his identity, he was unmoved. He smiled looking at the old man and said, "I have been running away from you my entire life. You have been my alter reality. I have been the Disturbance throughout and you the Calmness of this moment. I was riding the hands, while you have been on the dial always, unmoved, unaging, immortal!

You wanted to show me the true essence of time

right in the beginning, seventy years back, but I could only see Disturbance, hence the watch you gave me reflected my state of mind. And now, when I was ready for the truth, it stopped, making me one with reality, one with you, one with calmness, one with the dial."

He stretched his arm towards the old man, who too in turn extended his hand. Pedro slowly closed his eyes. The moment the two hands touched at the fingers, Pedro could feel a spark coming from the sky moving into his body through the touch. Every cell of his body was vibrating, while his mind had come into a state of ultimate calmness as if he had become one with the moment, one with the universe.

The calmness led him into a heavenly sleep. It was the longest sleep he had ever had, never wanting to wake up. No dreams, no disturbance, just plain calmness.

When he woke up, he was seated in the position where he had seen the old man, amongst the missing stones of the structure.

Was it a dream or reality?

It was daybreak now. The sunrays were hitting his eyes directly, yet there was pleasantness that he could feel, as if he were still in a state of serenity.

He saw a kid jumping in the center of the stone structure, shouting, "I am time! I am time!"

Pedro walked towards him. The kid got so scared looking at Pedro approaching him that he almost froze at that place.

Pedro went closer to him and handed over his watch to the kid, wanting to tell him the real meaning of time. He placed the watch in his hand and told him, 'This is your time.'

The watch, which hadn't been working till then, started ticking the moment it touched the kid's palm. The hands started moving. The kid was still a little shocked and so was Pedro.

Just then Pedro heard someone call out. "Pedro. Pedro." He could see a couple at the far end of the road with a man behind them working on a broken car. "Come here," the man shouted. The kid instantly turned and started running towards them.

Pedro smiled and walked away, realizing that he had stepped from the hands to the dial of time.

Every end merges with the beginning giving a sense of infinity to the finite events it withholds!